Nature's MINIBEASTS

Cockroaches

Clint Twist

GARETH**STEVENS**

PUBLISHING

A Member of the WRC Media Family of Companies

Please visit our web site at: www.garethstevens.com
For a free color catalog describing Gareth Stevens Publishing's list
of high-quality books and multimedia programs,
call 1-800-542-2595 (USA) or 1-800-387-3178 (Canada).
Gareth Stevens Publishing's fax: (414) 332-3567.

Library of Congress Cataloging-in-Publication Data

Twist, Clint.
    Cockroaches / Clint Twist. — North American ed.
      p. cm. — (Nature's minibeasts)
    Includes index.
    ISBN 08368-6373-9 (lib. bdg.)
    1. Cockroaches—Juvenile literature. I. Title.
  QL505.5.T85   2006
  595.7'28—dc22   2005054185

This North American edition first published in 2006 by
Gareth Stevens Publishing
A Member of the WRC Media Family of Companies
330 West Olive Street, Suite 100
Milwaukee, WI 53212 USA

This edition copyright © 2006 by Gareth Stevens, Inc. Original edition copyright © 2006
by ticktock Entertainment Ltd. First published in Great Britain in 2006 by ticktock Media Ltd.,
Unit 2, Orchard Business Centre, North Farm Road, Tunbridge Wells, Kent TN2 3XF.

Gareth Stevens series editor: Gini Holland
Gareth Stevens graphic designer: Dave Kowalski
Gareth Stevens art direction: Tammy West

Photo credits (t=top, b=bottom): Alamy: 5b (Paul Heartfield), 17 (James Caldwell), 20-21 (Bruce Coleman Inc.).
Ardea: 4 (Alan Weaving), 8b (Pat Morris). FLPA: 15 side panel, 21 side panel, 23 side panel (Nigel Cattlin),
5t (Mark Moffett/Minden Pictures), 7 side panel (Albert Mans/Foto Natura), 9, 13b, 19t (B. Borrell Casals).
Getty Images: 11 side panel (Burke/Triolo Productions). Nature Picture Library: 8 main (Nick Garbutt),
15 (Pete Oxford). The Natural History Museum, London: 23 middle. OSF: 3, 22 (Colin Milkins), 12
(Phototake Inc), 13t. Premaphotos Wildlife: 14l, 14-15, 19 side panel (Ken Preston-Mafham).
Science Photo Library: 11t (Barbera Strnadova), 16 (Volker Steger), 19b (Dr Morely Read), 21t (Jeff Lepore),
23t (Martin Dohrn), 27t (George Bernard).

Printed in the United States of America

1 2 3 4 5 6 7 8 9 10 09 08 07 06

Words that appear in the glossary are printed in
boldface type the first time they occur in text.

Contents

What Are Cockroaches? **4**

A Cockroach Up Close **6**

Unfussy Eaters **8**

Getting Around **10**

Finding Food **12**

Bad Habits **14**

Infrequent Flyers **16**

Egg Cases **18**

Nymph's Progress **20**

Cockroaches and Humans **22**

Unusual Behavior **24**

Sizes and Shapes **26**

Life Cycle **28**

Fabulous Facts **29**

Glossary **30**

Index **32**

What Are Cockroaches?

Cockroaches are winged **insects**. They like warm, damp, dirty places. Cockroaches can run very quickly. They are very tough and do not squash easily.

How do they live?

Cockroaches either live alone or in small family groups that include a female and her young. They are usually only seen at night.

This mountain cockroach mother cares for her young. They are about two hours old.

What do they eat?

Cockroaches will feed on just about any plant or animal material as long as it is already dead. Animals that live in this way are known

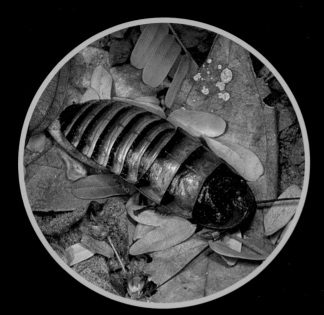

A Madagascan hissing cockroach walks along the forest floor.

Where do they live?

Cockroaches like to live in warm, damp conditions. Most cockroaches live in **tropical** and **subtropical** forests. Some kinds of cockroaches, however, have moved into human homes. Cockroaches are now found in cities all over the world.

Cockroaches love to eat **rotting** fruit.

UNDERSTANDING MINIBEASTS

Insects belong to a group of **minibeasts** known as **arthropods**. Adult arthropods have jointed legs, but they do not have inner **skeletons** made of bones. Instead, they have tough outer coverings, called **exoskeletons,** that support and protect their bodies. All insects have six legs when they are adults. Most insects also have at least one pair of wings. Some have two pairs.

Cockroaches have six legs and a tough exoskeleton.

A Cockroach Up Close

A cockroach is about ¾ to 1 ½ inches (2 to 4 centimeters) long and is reddish-brown in color. It has a tough outer covering that gives this minibeast a smooth, shiny look.

A dusky cockroach's head, close up, is not a pretty sight!

Beneath this covering, the cockroach has the same kind of body as all other adult insects. Its body is divided into three parts, which are the head, the **thorax**, and the **abdomen**.

The abdomen, the largest part of the cockroach's body, contains its digestive system.

The head has **antennae**, eyes, a mouth, and part of the brain. The rest of the brain is scattered along the underside of its body! Most insects have a mouth that points forward or downward, but a cockroach's mouth points backward, toward its body.

The head is often hidden from sight under a tough, protective shield.

The thorax is the middle part of the body, where the legs and wings are attached.

SIX LEGS

Beetles and other insects are sometimes called hexapods because they all have six legs (*hex* means six in Latin). This definition is correct, but it is not the whole story. All insects are hexapods, but not all hexapods are insects. Some other minibeasts, such as springtails, have six legs but they are not true insects.

Springtails (*above*) have six legs, but they are not insects. Cockroaches also have six legs, and they are insects.

Unfussy Eaters

Cockroaches are not just meat-eaters, and they are not just plant-eaters. These minibeasts will eat any kind of plant or animal food, but only if it is already dead.

This giant Madagascan hissing cockroach is eating rotting plants on the forest floor.

American cockroaches will eat animal droppings.

Cockroaches are not **predators** that hunt and kill other animals for food. Cockroaches are scavengers. They prefer their food to be not just dead, but decomposing, or **rotting**.

Decomposing occurs as **microbes**, known as **decomposers**, break down dead animals and plants.

An Oriental cockroach feeds on a dead insect.

Animals and plants turn soft and mushy as they rot. Cockroaches just love to eat this soft, mushy, partly rotten stuff. Most cockroaches will also feed on animal droppings.

Cockroaches are part of nature's clean-up crew. They help get rid of rotting animals, plants, and animal droppings.

LOG LIFE

Some cockroaches, known as wood roaches, feed on fallen trees. Wood, even rotten wood, is hard for most creatures to digest. Wood roaches are able to live on this poor diet, thanks to a particular microbe that lives in their digestive systems. Because of their special digestive systems, wood roaches do not have to go out in search of food. They can spend their lives safely inside a single rotten log.

A wood roach spends its whole life in a log, eating the rotting wood.

Getting Around

During the daytime, cockroaches hide from predators. Their flat bodies help these insects squeeze into the smallest hiding places, where they wait for darkness.

At night, cockroaches come out to feed. Although there are fewer predators around at night, the roaches still move very quickly. In fact, when it comes to walking and running, cockroaches are about the fastest things on six legs.

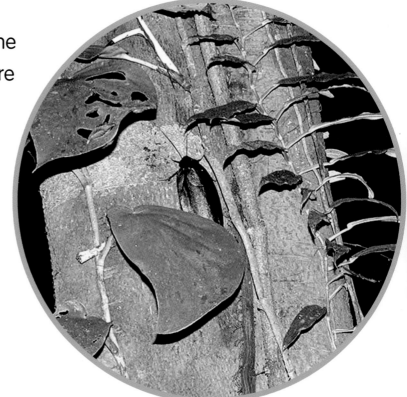

A cockroach walks the same way other insects walk. It lifts the middle leg on one side of its thorax at the same time as it lifts the front and back legs on the opposite side. In this way, it always has three legs touching the ground, which makes this insect well balanced and unlikely to fall over.

When cockroaches run, they do not change the pattern of their steps.

When cockroaches run, they really go fast! They lean back and lift the fronts of their bodies into the air so that they end up running on just their back legs. At full speed, some cockroaches can cover up to fifty body lengths per second, which is about ten times faster than a human runner.

To go from a walk to a run, insects just have to make their legs go faster. They do not have to change the pattern of their steps the way horses change from a walk to a gallop.

Cockroaches run on their back legs with great speed.

Horses use different patterns of steps, depending on how fast they want to go.

Finding Food

Cockroaches have very poor eyesight. Some of them can do little more than tell the difference between light and dark. They make up for this by having long antennae that have many sensitive **receptors**.

The antennae can bend well because they are divided into about one hundred **segments**. Each segment carries many sensitive receptors that the cockroach uses to find out about its surroundings.

The antennae on the head of this American cockroach are divided into about one hundred segments.

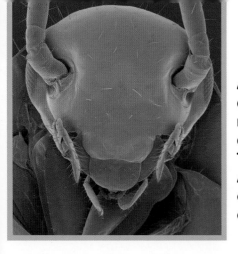

Antennae act as ears and noses as well as feelers. This is an American cockroach, close up.

Some receptors sense vibration. These receptors feel vibrations caused by movement. They also feel sound vibrations traveling through the air. Other receptors sense temperature. Cockroaches have separate receptors for hot and cold.

The most important receptors are those that let cockroaches sample smells. Different receptors sense different smells, especially smells made by rotting plants and animals.

An Oriental cockroach cleans its antennae.

In addition to their antennae, cockroaches can also sense vibrations through tiny bristles, or strong hairs, on their legs. Even while their antennae are searching for food, their legs are alert to any movements around them.

The hairs on a cockroach's leg can feel the smallest movement.

Cockroaches are not nice to be around. For one thing, cockroaches make a bad smell. No matter how bad the smells of rotting meat or plants are, cockroaches smell even worse.

Some cockroaches use their own smell as a self-defense weapon. If they are threatened by a predator, they can squirt out a cloud of foul-smelling liquid. When the predator runs from the bad smell, the cockroaches can easily escape.

Camouflage is another form of self-defense. This cockroach looks just like a dead leaf.

NEVER MIND THE SMELL

What makes cockroaches really bad neighbors, even to animals with no sense of smell, is the fact that they lack any form of toilet training. They leave a nonstop trail of droppings wherever they walk. Because their mouths point backward, cockroaches have to walk all over their food in order to eat it. They even leave droppings on food they have not eaten.

This cockroach's self-defense system failed. A scorpion is eating it up!

The bad smell a cockroach makes might be a message to other cockroaches saying, "Here is plenty of food." It might have the opposite meaning, saying "Keep away, this food is mine."

Whatever the meaning to other roaches, the message to other animals clearly says "Avoid this insect."

A German cockroach walks over food and leaves droppings.

These Australian cockroaches are feeding on a cake.

Infrequent Flyers

Both male and female cockroaches have wings, but the females of most cockroach species cannot fly. Only males have wings that can be used for flying, but they do not use them often.

Most of the time, male and female cockroaches live separate lives. At mating time, the females give off special smells, or scents, that are known as **pheromones**. These scents mix with the air and get carried away on the wind.

A male cockroach will use his antennae to detect a female.

Some of the smell receptors on the male cockroach's antennae can detect the smallest trace of the female's pheromones.

When female pheromones reach the male, he flies back toward the waiting female by following the invisible pheromone trail.

Two American cockroaches mate.

If the male cannot find the female right away, he lands and gives off his own pheromones. These are not as strong as the female's, but they act in the same way. They help the female find the male in the dark.

Most cockroaches cannot fly. This male American cockroach only flies to find a mate.

Not all minibeasts have to mate to produce young. Some insect species, such as the Surinam roach, are all female. They can produce fertile eggs without the need for any males.

The Surinam roach does not need a male to **reproduce**.

Egg Cases

There are over four thousand kinds of cockroaches. After mating, most female cockroaches lay their eggs inside special egg cases. Depending on the species of cockroach, six to fifty eggs can be found neatly arranged in an egg case.

Some types of cockroaches carry their egg cases around with them for a few days before leaving them in dark, damp places. Other kinds of cockroaches, however, continue to carry their egg cases. They will carry them up to several weeks until their eggs hatch.

This smoky brown cockroach's egg case shows the seam on the bottom edge.

All cockroach egg cases have an outer surface which is smooth and leathery, with a raised seam, called a keel, along one edge. Tiny openings at the bottom of the keel allow the eggs inside to breathe.

An Oriental cockroach carries its egg case.

Only a few types of cockroaches do not lay eggs at all. Instead, their eggs develop inside the females' abdomens. The young cockroaches, called **nymphs**, are born alive and not laid as eggs.

A female cockroach gives birth to her young, or nymphs.

INSECT DEVELOPMENT

Insects develop from eggs in two different ways. With many kinds of insects, including cockroaches and grasshoppers, the eggs hatch into nymphs that already have their adult body shapes. With many other kinds of insects, such as bees and beetles, the eggs hatch into **larvae** that look very different from the adults. The larvae then go through a stage called **pupation**, when they change into adults.

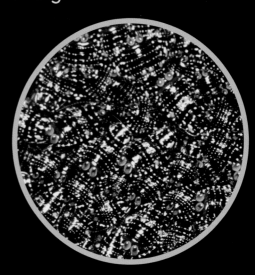

These cockroach nymphs pack closely together.

Nymph's Progress

Young cockroach nymphs look like tiny copies of the adults. Nymphs can take up to ten months to become full adults. During this time, these youngsters will shed their exoskeletons a number of times.

This nymph has just shed its exoskeleton, which looks like a white cockroach.

Each insect has an exoskeleton that supports and protects its body. Exoskeletons are strong and tough, but they do not stretch. When it starts to grow too big for its exoskeleton, the nymph must grow a new one before it can shed the old one.

An cockroach nymph looks adult.

An eastern milk snake sheds its skin.

With each molt, nymphs become more complete. For example, newly hatched nymphs have no wings, and their antennae have only about twenty-five segments, compared to about one hundred segments on adult antennae. Until the nymph reaches its final stage of growth, its wings and antennae will not work as well as an adult's.

The act by which an animal sheds its outer covering is known as **molting**. Insects and other arthropods are not the only animals that molt. Some animals that have internal skeletons, such as snakes, also shed their skins as they grow.

Newly hatched cockroach nymphs are pale and almost colorless, but they soon begin to turn darker. The youngsters will go through as many as twelve molts before they are fully adult.

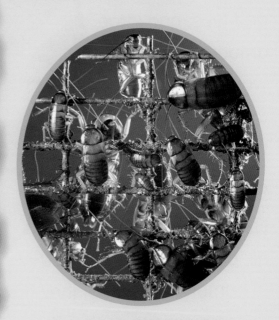
Adult and nymph American cockroaches climb together.

Cockroaches and Humans

Cockroaches are most at home in warm, wet woodlands, but, a long time ago, they found that human homes are equally inviting.

Houses that are set up to be comfortable for people are also comfortable for cockroaches. Human homes provide everything the roaches need, including heat, dampness in sinks and tubs, and large amounts of organic waste, which is unwanted bits of plants and animals.

Some cockroach species, about twenty in all, are so closely attached to human homes that they have become serious pests. These cockroaches are now found in almost every town and city in the world.

Many cockroaches find humans are great sources of food and water.

Some of the worst pests are the Oriental, the American, and the German cockroaches. These insects are often found living under floors and between walls, especially in bathrooms and kitchens, where they find water, waste, and garbage.

The German cockroach actually comes from Africa.

The Oriental cockroach likes damp places.

The American cockroach is a terrible pest.

SPOILERS

Cockroaches are pests, not only because of the food they eat, but also because of the food they spoil. They crawl all over their food and scatter their droppings as they go. In fact, cockroaches spoil much more food than they actually eat. Wherever they live, they make a smelly mess.

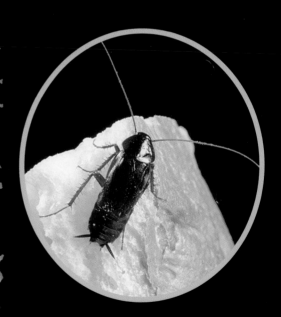

An Oriental cockroach crawls over, and spoils, a piece of bread.

Unusual Behavior

Some cockroaches do fairly surprising things. Not only can the largest species grow to an amazing 3 inches (7 cm), but the fastest cockroaches are entered into races by their human owners.

Hissing Monster

The Madagascan giant cockroach is one of the biggest roaches, at about 3 inches (7 cm) in length. It is also the noisiest. In fact, it is so noisy that it uses sound as a weapon to defend itself. When this cockroach is disturbed, it repeatedly puffs its body up with air and then huffs the air out through tiny openings on its body surface. The air makes a loud hissing sound as it comes out. This sound is often enough to scare predators, giving the giant cockroach time to escape.

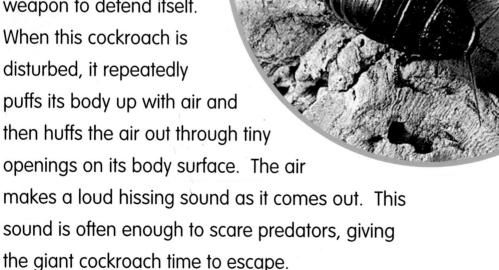

Parental Care

Most young cockroaches do not get any care from their parents. New wood roach nymphs, however, must stay with their mother. When these nymphs hatch, they do not have the microbes that let them feed on wood. At first, the nymphs have to stay close to their mother and feed on her droppings. These droppings contain the microbes which allow the roaches to feed on wood. Only after several weeks do these nymphs have enough of the microbes to start feeding on wood.

Fast Runners

Many cockroaches can run fairly quickly, but none are faster than the American cockroach. This amazing insect can cover a distance of 59 inches (150 cm) in one second, which is about five times faster than a German cockroach, which can only cover about 12 inches (30 cm) in one second.

Cockroach Sport

In some places, cockroach racing is a sport. Races are run in daylight around a circular track. According to the rules, roaches that do not start running right away may be poked and prodded into action.

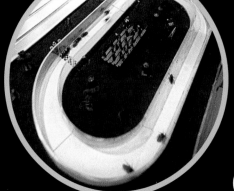

Sizes and Shapes

Although most cockroaches have the same basic body parts, they show much variety in shape, size, and color.

Leaf Cockroach

This West African cockroach hides from daytime predators by standing on the forest floor and keeping very still. It is well hidden because it looks like a fallen yellow leaf, complete with one area that looks as though it is turning brown.

Tropical Giant Cockroach

This cockroach from the tropical forests of Central America is one of the largest cockroaches in the world. When fully grown, it can measure more than 3 inches (7.5 cm) in length.

Banana Roach

The green banana roach does not invade houses, but it is a pest because it feeds on crops.

Cape Mountain Roach

The Cape Mountain cockroach lives in highland forests near the southern tip of Africa. Unlike most cockroaches, this cockroach does not lay its eggs in an egg case. Instead, the eggs stay inside the female's body until the nymphs hatch.

Life Cycle

Most female cockroaches lay their eggs in a special case. The eggs hatch into nymphs, which molt about twelve times before becoming fully grown adults. At least one kind of cockroach does not lay eggs, but gives birth to nymphs, instead.

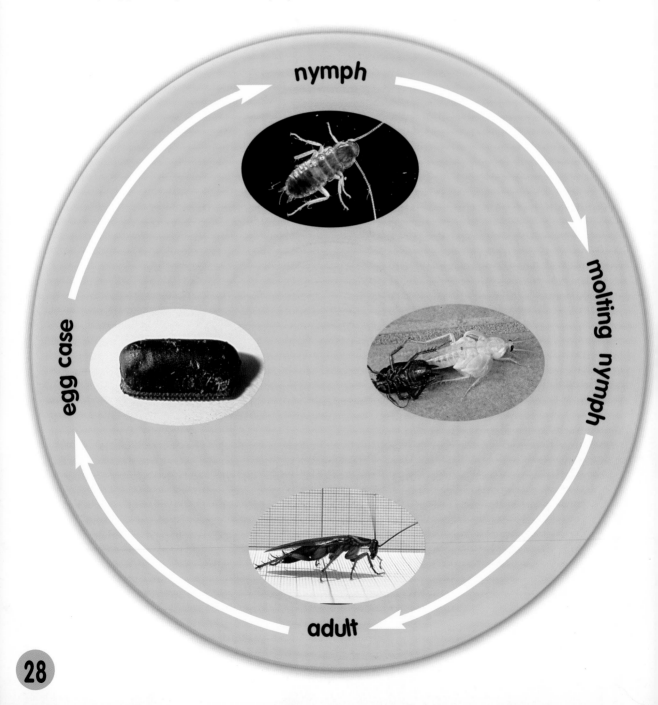

nymph

molting nymph

egg case

adult

Fabulous Facts

Fact 1: Cockroaches breathe through holes in their sides called spiracles.

Fact 2: Cockroaches cannot see in red light, but they can see very well in green light.

Fact 3: Cockroaches get their sense of smell from their antennae.

Fact 4: A cockroach mouth moves from side to side, not up and down the way human mouths do.

Fact 5: Cockroaches can live up to two years.

Fact 6: Some humans are allergic to cockroaches. Some people get asthma attacks from being around cockroaches.

Fact 7: If a cockroach's head is cut off, it can survive for up to a week, and then only dies of thirst. It survives this long because its brain is scattered along the underside of its body, which means that cutting off its head does not kill all of its brain.

Fact 8: Cockroaches have been present on Earth for more than four hundred million years.

Fact 10: Most cockroaches have a total of eighteen knees on their six legs.

Fact 11: Some kinds of cockroaches can hold their breath for forty minutes.

Fact 12: Cockroaches thrive in nearly every corner of the globe, in spite of people's best efforts to get rid of them.

Fact 13: Cockroaches' eyes are made up of four thousand lenses. This large number of lenses allows cockroaches to see in all directions at the same time.

Glossary

abdomen — the largest part of an insect's three-part body, which holds most of its important organs

antenna/antennae — a pair of sense organs found at the front of the head on most insects. One half of that pair is called an antenna.

arthropods — minibeasts that have jointed legs, including insects, spiders, scorpions, mites, and ticks

camouflage — the means used to hide by looking or acting like something else

decomposers — microscopic plants and animals that break down the dead bodies of other plants and animals

digestive system — the organs in the bodies of animals that are used to process food

exoskeletons — hard outer coverings that protect and support the bodies of some minibeasts that do not have inner skeletons

insects — kinds of minibeasts that have six legs, a body with three parts, and, in most cases, one or more pairs of wings

larva/ larvae — the worm-like form of an insect after it hatches from an egg. More than one larva are called larvae.

microbes — tiny living germs that are so small that they can only been seen through a powerful microscope

minibeast — one of a large number of small land animals that do not have a skeleton, including insects, spiders, mites, and scorpions

molting — the process of shedding the body's surface layer, such as an insect's exoskeleton or a snake's skin, so that it can be replaced by a new, larger one

nymphs — the young forms of those insects that do not produce larvae

pheromones — scent substances, used to communicate and attract mates, that are produced by many kinds of animals, including humans

predators — animals that hunt, kill, and then eat other animals

pupation — the process by which insect larvae change their body shape to the adult form

receptors — tiny organs that detect things such as smell, heat, and vibration

rotting — the process by which the bodies of dead animals and plants are broken down into dirt, or compost

scavengers — animals that eat dead and rotting plants and animals

segments — pieces that link together to form one larger unit, such as inches on a ruler or sections of an insect's antenna

skeletons — inner structures of bones that support the bodies of many large animals

subtropical — belonging to a region near the tropics, where it is warm

thorax — the middle part of an insect's body where the legs are attached

tropical — belonging to the region on and along either side of Earth's equator, where the climate is hot

Index

abdomens 5, 6, 19
adults   5, 6, 19, 20,
     21, 28
African cockroaches   26, 27
American cockroaches
     8, 12, 13, 17, 21, 23, 25
antennae 7, 12, 13, 16, 21, 29
arthropods 5, 21
Australian cockroaches 14, 15

banana roaches 27
brains 7, 29

clean-up insects 9

decomposers 9
defense systems
     14, 15, 24
digestive systems 6, 9
droppings 8, 9, 15, 23, 25

egg cases 18, 19, 27, 28
exoskeletons 5, 20
eyes 7, 12, 29

family groups 4
females 4, 16, 17, 19, 28
flying 16, 17
food 4, 5, 8, 9, 12,
     14, 15, 22, 23
forests 5, 27

German cockroaches 15, 23, 25
giant cockroaches 8, 24, 27

heads 6, 7, 29
hexapods 7
hissing 24
humans 5, 11, 22, 23, 24, 29

insects 5, 10, 17, 19,
     20, 21

larva/larvae 19
leaf cockroaches 26
legs 5, 7, 10, 11, 13
life cycles 28, 29
light 29

Madagascan cockroaches
     5, 8, 24
males 16, 17
mating 16, 17, 18
microbes 9, 25
minibeasts 5
     see also insects
molting 21, 28
mountain cockroaches 4
mouths 7, 15, 29

night 4, 10
nymphs 19, 20, 21, 25, 27, 28

Oriental cockroaches 9, 13, 19, 23

pests 22, 23, 27
pheromones 16, 17
predators 9, 10, 14, 15, 24, 26
pupation 19

racing cockroaches 24, 25
receptors 12, 13, 16
running 10, 11, 25

skeletons 5, 21
smells 13, 14, 15, 29
smoky brown cockroaches 18
springtails 7
Surinam roaches 17

thoraxes 6, 7

walking 10, 11
wings 5, 7, 16, 17, 21
wood roaches 9, 25